KT-157-738

Hubble-Bubble

by the same author

THE TRUMPET IN THE HALL
WAVELL: Portrait of a Soldier
THE WATERY MAZE
RUPERT OF THE RHINE (Brief Lives)
THE BLACK WATCH AND THE KING'S ENEMIES
THE WILD GREEN EARTH
BEYOND THE CHINDWIN
RETURN TO BURMA

ETON PORTRAIT

CAPTAIN JOHN NIVEN (Novel)
THE RARE ADVENTURE (Novel)

LOWLAND SOLDIER (verse)

This book is to be returned on or before

Hubble-Bubble

BERNARD FERGUSSON

Drawings by Charles Gore

STIRLING
DISTRICT
LIBRARY

COLLINS St James's Place, London 1978

B 4

William Collins Sons & Co. Ltd
London · Glasgow · Sydney · Auckland
Toronto · Johannesburg

821
FER

First published 1978
© Bernard Fergusson 1978
ISBN 0 00 211378 3
Set in Monotype Garamond
Made and printed in Great Britain by
William Collins Sons & Co. Ltd, Glasgow

Foreword

Once upon a time, in the 1930s, I was an impecunious subaltern with expensive tastes and the habit of scribbling frivolous and ephemeral verses. One day I discovered, to my astonishment, that the latter could sometimes be sold for guineas to subsidize the former.

The occasional cheque from *Punch*, for which I was soon writing prose as well as verse, was more than a godsend: it was a bacon-saver, helping me to meet my mess-bills and other commitments. For verse, *Punch* used to pay 2s. 6d. a line: a lot of money in those days, when a subaltern's pay was 9s. 10d. a day.

From the habit of scribbling verse I never recovered; and I was surprised lately to find how much of what I had perpetrated had survived and accumulated. Here is a selection, in roughly chronological order.

I recall with gratitude the kindness and encouragement I had from E. V. Knox ('Evoe') and Kenneth Bird ('Fougasse') during their respective editorships. More than twenty of the pieces that I have resurrected in this book made their first appearance in *Punch*, and I offer my thanks to the present Editor, Mr Alan Coren, and the Proprietors, for their permission to reprint them.

Contents

November Reflections

In those far-off, pre-war days, officers were expected to hunt, whether they liked it or not: not only was it 'the done thing', but it was also supposed to endow you with 'an eye for country'. I never cared for it, and furthermore could barely afford it; but one was allowed to borrow a horse from the Army for the mere amount of its insurance (fifteen shillings a week, hence the phrase 'a fifteen-bobber') with its Army groom. I kitted myself out with second-hand clothes, and hunted like a good, though not very happy, boy for several seasons.

I would fain
Hunt this season once again.
Well and good; but is my kit
        Fit?

    Years of wear
Show upon it here and there
In the form of brilliant green
        Sheen.

    I should say
All I'd get for it today
Is a tanner at the pop-
        Shop.

    And I doubt
If I really dare go out
In that coat, or even that
        Hat.

    Even the breeches
Have an odd appearance, which is
Reminiscent of a shabby
        Cabby.

    None the less,
Hunt I shall till strain and stress
Burst the seams, and I am un-
        Done:

    In which case,
First abandoning the chase,
I shall simply have to hack
        Back.

On the Death of a
Favourite Cockatoo

Gentlemen, let's
Sing a dirge to the sweetest of pets,
Perished on Friday in spite of a couple of vets.

Not from old age,
Gout, apoplexy or rage;
Not from impatience at being shut up in a cage;

Not from a bite
Sustained in the course of a fight;
Not even from grief or from having a pain in the night:

Nothing like those
Caused her to turn up her toes
And carried her off to wherever a cockatoo goes.

Born Martinique,
She was always patrician and *chic*
From the tip of her elegant tail to the end of her beak.

Nevertheless
Her husband succumbed to distress
Due to her pinching his share of the mustard and cress.

Early and late
She pined for her consort and mate,
Till it seemed that herself she would share his
                                                    unfortunate fate.

Knowing the ropes,
To banish her fit of the mopes
We filled up her cage with small birds, and were living
                                    in hopes

Watching them thrive,
Thinking they'd keep her alive,
Till within a few minutes we found that she'd eaten all
                                    five.

                    ★

Somewhere afar,
Her spirit shines out like a star,
Having died like a Queen of a surfeit of budgerigar.

The Sacrifice

In point of fact, it was at the Royal Tournament of 1934, and not the Aldershot Tattoo, that The Black Watch was detailed to stage an historical Pageant. One of the scenes represented the inspection of the Regiment before the Battle of Fontenoy in 1743 by the Duke of Cumberland. It fell to me to take the part of the Duke, and I was ordered to shave off the moustache which I had worn ever since my last year at school. Among those who saw the show in London were King George V and Queen Mary; and when later we took it on to Edinburgh 'The Duke of Cumberland' had to be given police protection from militant Scottish Nationalists, armed with tomatoes.

O Ichabod, O Ichabod! the glory is departed.
Forgive my incoherence, but I don't know what to do.
They've taken my moustache away and I am broken-
hearted:
They wouldn't let me wear it in the Aldershot Tattoo.

They bribed me with a wig and with the glories of the
pageant;
They said it wasn't suited to the eighteenth century;
They said its loss would spoil my looks far less than I
imagined,
Though I was so attached to it, and it attached to me.

Right nobly the condemned moustache still twirled
throughout the morning,
Right gallant was its bearing in an atmosphere of
gloom:
Then, for the last and final time my countenance
adorning,
It went with me without reproach but proudly to its
doom.

The barber clipped it once and twice and lathered it and
shaved it,
And all my crowning glory lay about me on the floor;
But now the situation's saved – my sacrifice has saved
it –
And the anachronism now need trouble us no more.

About me in the ring shall flash the halberd and the
claymore;
Bewigged and glorious I shall move to my appointed
place;
But this I swear: I'll not remain clean-shaven for a day
more
Than need be till I right the wrong I did upon my
face.

A Subaltern to his Father on an Important Occasion (1934)

My father took slight, but happily passing, umbrage when he read in *Punch* what he took to be a reflection upon the contents of his cellar; but he accepted my explanation that this was purely poetic licence, and the occasion was duly celebrated on my next leave home.

You see
In me
A happy man!
I hide
My pride
As best I can.
Today
You may
Congratulate
Your son
Upon
His new estate.

A bust,
I trust!
Come, when we dine,
I think
We'll drink
The '99.
Our port
Is short,
But let it rip:
'My health
And wealth,
My Second Pip.'

The Modern A.D.C.

In March, 1935, I joined Major-General A. P. Wavell at
Aldershot, who had just been appointed to command the 2nd
Infantry Division there, as his first-ever A.D.C. This was a
turning-point in my life: since I was to serve him – the greatest
officer that The Black Watch has produced in all its long
history – several times thereafter both in peace and war, in
every rank from Lieutenant to Lieutenant-Colonel, on the
staff and in the field. He was himself no mean hand at pro-
ducing light verse, and during my two years with him at
Aldershot he used to rejoice with me when *Punch* accepted my
offerings, and condole with me when they didn't. Here is one
that *Punch* accepted and Wavell relished:

I am the very model of a modern A.D.C.:
There's no one hands the sherry round so gracefully as
                         me.
My manners are impeccable, my dignity is such as is
Supposed to be the perquisite of dowagers and
                         duchesses.
No fashionable popinjay, no sugar-king or banker-chief
Can rival me in tie or tails or buttonhole or handkerchief.
My conversation ranges with authoritative bonhomie
From Problems of the Army to Political Economy.
If stumped, I only murmur: 'Well, it wouldn't be
                         discreet to say:'
And if my audience demurs, I answer: 'That's for me to
                         say.'
The more that I consider it, the more it seems to me
I am the very model of the modern A.D.C.

I never talk to subalterns or captains – it's undignified;
I never talk to anyone as if I thought they signified:
I hurry past the smaller fry, and only to the big adhere
(I never talk to anyone below the rank of Brigadier).
I never ride in uniform: my boots are not intended for
Equestrian exercise at all, but office work they're
                                      splendid for.
I spend manoeuvres in a car, for in a limousine it is
Not only much more dignified, but nearer one's
                                      amenities.
I sleep in village inns, of course: a fellow doesn't care
                                      about
A bivouac – it's draughty, and it's apt to blow your
                                      hair about.
I've thought about it thoroughly: it's obvious to me
I am the very model of a modern A.D.C.

In short, when I've descended from the theory to the
                                      practical,
And learnt the principles of war, strategical and
                                      tactical;
When I can march for thirty miles on heather or on
                                      tarmac, or
Have learnt to handle a platoon as ably as an Army
                                      Corps;
When I have learnt my job a bit, and needn't feel an ass
                                      if I
Am given dinners to inspect, or riflemen to classify;
When I'm reduced to cadging, or endeavouring to
                                    cadge, a tent,
And saying: 'Yes, Sir,' 'No, Sir,' 'If you please, Sir,' to
                                    an adjutant;
When I can do the duties of an ordinary officer
As well as saying: 'Sherry?' or, 'Some brandy with your
                                    coffee, Sir?'
I'll be a soldier then; but now it's quite enough for me
To be the very model of a modern A.D.C.

A Farewell to Flying

The future Field-Marshal Lord Wavell was immensely air-minded from his early youth, and had flown operational sorties in 1915 without permission, as observer to a friend and brother-officer of his in The Black Watch, 'Biffy' Borton. He did his level best, far in advance of his contemporaries, to make the British Army air-minded. Such experiments as were being made were very tentative; but he was much impressed by the potential of low-winged monoplanes, with short take-offs and landings, and by the auto-gyro, the fore-runner of the helicopter. Not only did he himself use them as much as he was allowed to – and indeed more – he used to send me on errands hither and yon in one or other of these machines, to demonstrate their excellence in the rôle of liaison. The verses that follow are wholly devoid of fact, except for the precautions taken; and they omit all reference to the invariable hospitality of No. 4 (Army Co-operation) Royal Air Force Squadron, before, during and after these flights.

> Kind stranger, take me home:
> I do not like this aerodrome.
> They knew I was only a simple tyro,
> But they sent me up in an auto-gyro.
>
> As soon as I reached the place
> They togged me up like a flying ace;
> Even now my imagination boggles
> To think what I wore in the way of goggles.
>
> They gave me a flying-suit,
> And trussed me up in a parachute,
> And told me straight, if it didn't function,
> They wouldn't expect me back to luncheon.

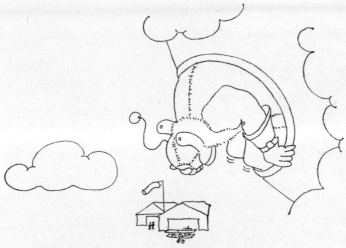

They made me sign a chit
To say (and I didn't think much of it)
If I went a-missing while *in excelsis*
It was all my fault, and nobody else's.

They put me into a seat
And said I wasn't to move my feet;
They said: 'Shut up!' when I hadn't spoken,
Except to tell them my belt was broken.

Before we left the ground,
The thing on the top went round and round:
I tried to get out before we sped off,
And the thing damn nearly took my head off.

It only remains to tell
To what extent I was far from well:
I was sick as a dog, to be perfectly candid,
From the time we left to the time we landed.

So, Stranger! take me home!
I do not like this aerodrome.
I shan't be coming again – far from it:
I'm the dog that doesn't return to his vomit.

Protest Evoked by a Night Operation

These lines were inspired, if that is the word, by a particularly unpleasant and very wet twenty-four-hour manoeuvre in 1935. By an unfortunate lapse of memory, I substituted the name 'Atalanta' for the 'Arethusa' of Swinburne's original; and it was 'Atalanta' that appeared in *Punch*. I received a reproachful note from the then editor E. V. Knox: 'Why, O why, did you write "Atalanta"? And why, O why, did we print it?'

Arethusa arose from her bed in the snows
    Of the Acroceraunian mountains,
And I from a bed on a bleak watershed
    When the heavens are spouting like fountains;
And I very much fear that the moment is near
    When, as surely as I am a sinner,
They will tell me to fight for the rest of the night,
    And then run seven miles for my dinner.

It was all very well for that slip of a gel
    If to sleep in the snow was her liking,
And I do not deny that in Greece in July
    There is pleasure in running and hiking;
But I'm blowed if I see why a fellow like me,
    No more in his physical heyday,
Must needs emulate at the whim of the State
    An Acroceraunian lady.

Dress Regulations

In about 1936 the fashion began to creep in of playing tennis in shorts as opposed to trousers. This daring innovation was frowned on by the Old Guard, and the Committee of the Officers' Club at Aldershot ordained that, whereas shorts might be worn on the actual courts, they were banned from the Club-house. I perpetrated the following verses in *Punch*. They were perforce anonymous, since I had not then achieved the distinction of being allowed to append my initials: a privilege which in those days was restricted to those who had graduated as established and regular contributors. But everybody in the intimate world of Aldershot credited me with the authorship; and at the next meeting of the Committee it was moved, and carried by a small majority, that I should be expelled from the Club for my temerity. The anti-climax came when the Secretary, producing the list of members so as to expunge my name, was obliged to reveal to the Committee that I wasn't, and never had been, a member. The brutal truth was that I had never been able to afford the subscription.

Licentious and brutal they call us in war,
    But nevertheless we uphold the proprieties
Even more strictly than ever before.
    Lend us your ears and approve what our fiat is:
As from today, we've decided that Nemesis
Overtakes all who wear shorts on the premises.

    Come in your uniform, come in your rags,
        Come in your tweeds if you think you look nice
                        in them,
    Come in pyjamas or grey flannel bags;
      But come in your shorts and you'll never come
                        twice in them:
    Be you a General or merely a Subaltern,
    Even the worms on the lawn of the Club'll turn.

Britons have always been known to combine
  A great reputation for hardy and dressy men;
Even in the jungle we dress when we dine,
  Save for a rare and untypical specimen,
Yet there's an element who in their folly would
Rival the rig-out of Marlene and Hollywood.

We are the leaders of fashion, the hub
  Of decent Society, civil and military:
Shall it be said that the Officers' Club
  Failed in its duty of rousing the dilatory?
Others have followed from time immemorial
Where we have led them in matters sartorial.

Now we have acted, I firmly believe
  The danger is over, and people can breathe again;
Doomed is the fashion of Adam and Eve,
  Of those who would have us revert to a wreath again.
All that is needed is strictness awhile and a
Chucker-out able to deal with a Highlander.

  Come in your uniform, come in plus-fours,
    Come in the corduroy trousers you beagle in,
  Come in your waders or come in jodhpurs,
    Come in those knee-breeches footmen look regal in.
  This is your Club: you may do as you please in it,
  Always provided you don't shew your knees in it.

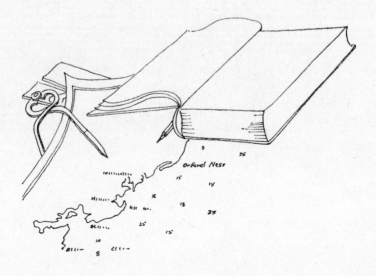

Orford Ness

The Ship's Fly

(AN EPIC OF THE HIGHLAND BRIGADE
YACHT CLUB)

The Highland Brigade Yacht Club was established in 1935, and evaporated sadly during the course of the ensuing war, when all its members were scattered far and wide: it never rose again. But for four happy years it flourished; and its pride and joy was the 33-ton gaff-rigged ex-Bristol Channel pilot cutter *Saladin*, a truly noble vessel and a splendid keeper of the seas in hard weather, which we managed to buy cheap and to run on a financial shoe-string. Perhaps her most glorious hours under the Highland Brigade burgee were those spent in the Fastnet Race of 1937; but her voyage north from Ipswich to Grangemouth in the Firth of Forth in 1936, which we did in 48 hours thanks to a spanking south-westerly, Force 5 to 6, remains an equally happy memory. So does our unforeseen ship-mate.

He wasn't upon the articles as a member of the crew;
He wasn't upon the Passenger List so far as the Owner
knew;
He must have boarded the yacht, we think, as she lay
beside the quay,
But he didn't declare his presence there till two days
out to sea.

We discovered him first off Orfordness; I don't know
where he slept,
But we found him at a clandestine meal in the place
where the jam was kept;
And he seemed to buzz: 'I know you're bound from
Ipswich to the Forth:
Well, I'm sorry to say I'm a stowaway, but I'll work my
passage north.'

Day by day we'd a following wind, and it looked like a
record trip;
The new recruit to the starboard watch was the life and
soul of the ship.
In all the duties of shipboard life he willingly played
his part,
And he helped the skipper to navigate by walking
about the chart.

He'd a fine contempt for the Haisborough Bank and the
Cork and the Middle Sand;
He walked impartially over the sea and flew all over the
land;
He studied the charts and the almanacks, the
chronometer and the sextant,
And read each Notice to Mariners that he considered
extant.

But our ship-mate at last grew overbold: he thought we
should sail him faster;
His buzz grew insubordinate as he criticized the Master;
He raided a pot of marmalade, and inspired by such
carousing
He left the ship for the NNW, on a course for the
Outer Dowsing.

Alas for his over-confidence! My ship-mates think it
plain
That the fly of the good ship *Saladin* will never be seen
again.
It may be the gulfs have washed him down far short of
Flamborough Head,
But can it be that such as he is really and truly dead?

Often now in the Middle Watch I scan the angry sea,
And I find my heart and my thoughts go out to my
                    ship-mate's Odyssey.
Does he sojourn now in a boarding-house in an East
                    Coast seaside town,
Or is he far 'neath an alien star, still running the
                    westing down?

Even now he may come again, winging his way in the
                    dark
With a little marmalade in his beak, like the dove to
                    Noah's Ark.
Leave the fore-hatch wide: there's a fatted calf (in the
                    shape of jam) within,
For the rapturous day when our stowaway comes back
                    to *Saladin*!

Lament for a Wisdom Tooth

This tragedy befell me in 1936 in Edinburgh, where I was a member of a large and – but for me in my agony – jolly house party for the annual Highland Ball. But I was as jolly as anybody once the tragedy had been enacted. For some reason, *Punch* chose to publish the verses in its Summer Number of that year, which was otherwise a cheerful publication.

> Come, let us mourn my wisdom tooth!
>   This afternoon we twain were parted
> (Although I'm not, to tell the truth,
>   Precisely broken-hearted:
> The pain of the bereavement comes
> Less from the heart than from the gums).

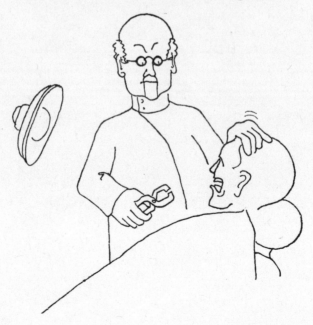

Nevertheless we two were one
    Until the dentist's shrewd inspection
Shortly before the deed was done
    That severed our connection.
Such was its friendship with my tongue,
At least it shall not die unsung.

No ordinary tooth was mine,
    And I shall miss it not a little.
It had a pretty taste in wine,
    It chewed a pretty victual:
My only claim to fame in youth
Was for the sweetness of my tooth.

The dentist looked at it askance;
    It looked at him, it looked pathetic.
Unmoved, he put it in a trance
    With local anaesthetic.
'Now then!' he said; 'hold tight! I'll git him!'
He did; but not before it bit him.

So died this tooth of sapience,
    And now I feel extremely tender
Towards the yawning cavern whence
    At last it made surrender:
I never thought the little chap
Would leave behind him such a gap.

That tooth, which used to hold in store
    Wisdom more sharp than Aristotle,
I shall preserve for evermore
    Within a spirit-bottle:
So shall posterity inherit
My tooth alike in flesh and spirit.

To My First Grey Hair

This grisly discovery
befell me in 1938, when
I was posted from Palestine
to be the French instructor
at Sandhurst, the only
subaltern on the staff there.

All Heil! my new yet venerable Hair!
   (I greet you as a German would an Aryan
In Tel Aviv). Amazed, I stand and stare
    Silent, as though upon a peak in Darien.
      Amazed I stand
         And seek my wits to gather,
      My razor in my hand,
         My face all lather.

Amazed, but not with shock or pain or rage.
   To tell the truth, I'm feeling rather gratified,
As one who sought a covenant with Age
   And unexpectedly has found it ratified.
      Why should I swear
         And make my head do penance
      When it has made me rare
         Among Lieutenants?

Rare as an Aryan in Tel Aviv
  Are grey-haired subalterns. They'll think my
                                  knowledge is
Up to the form, I readily believe,
  Required for entry to our two Staff Colleges.
    Certain I am
      That now I ought to get a
    Place on the list for Cam-
      berley or Quetta.

And so, since it has taken you, mein herr,
  More than a quarter-century to reveal yourself.
When next I venture to the barber's chair
  I do beseech you carefully to conceal yourself.
    What would I do
      If an ill-omened morrow
    Should really bring you to
      The grave in sorrow?

Perish the thought! I will not contemplate
  Even for a moment the resultant agonies;
Who could envisage such a fearful fate?
  Hitched to your star alone my humble wagon is.
    On you be peace!
      On you my constant blessing!
    But *not* on you be grease
      Or patent dressing.

Wider be your dominion on my head,
  Where other hairs (mouse-coloured, with a dull
                            tip) lie;
Broader and farther be your kingdom spread;
  Be grey, be fruitful still, and multiply.
    Let others book
      Scalp-massage or a lotion:
    To you alone I look
      For my promotion.

On a Friend Married at Bath 1939

Look to your flanks
    And keep your powder dry;
Close, bachelors, your ranks
    Or worse than die!
A monstrous regiment
    Of bits of fluff
Is hot upon the scent
    And powder-puff.

The ladies yet
    May like the heathen rage:
I am escaped their net
    And past the age.
Wind-swept or permed –
    I have no wish to mate,
A bachelor confirmed
    At twenty-eight.

Nevertheless,
    Some other men there be
Who do not quite possess
    Such constancy.
Should we deny to men
    Of weaker clay
Some meed of pity when
    They fall away?

Nay: mourn him who
    Incontinently met
His field of Waterloo
    In Somerset;
Who – tell it not in Gath –
    Threw up the sponge,
And stole away to Bath
    To take the plunge.

Ode on the Retirement of the Permanent Under-Secretary of State for War

Sir Herbert Creedy (1878–1973) was Private Secretary to no fewer than seven Secretaries of State for War, including Asquith, Kitchener, Lloyd George and Churchill, and then head of the War Office from 1920 to 1939. Up till the outbreak of war, every officer used to receive individually

through the post flimsy printed sheets known as Army Council Instructions, dealing with incredibly detailed *minutiae*, the contents of which he was required to master. He was also liable to be called upon to produce for inspection the whole series, amended and brought up to date. The usual practice, in my own Regiment at any rate, was to pay a retainer to one of the junior clerks in the Battalion Orderly Room to perform this latter, loathsome chore on one's behalf, out of the nine shillings and tenpence *per diem* which constituted a 2/Lieutenant's pay in those days, a sum which fell short of satisfying even the most modest mess bill. These communications were signed 'H. J. Creedy' in facsimile; or, in his temporary absence, by his No. 2, one H. J. Widdows. I can see both these signatures in my mind's eye to this day.

Creedy and Widdows retired within a few months of each other in 1939: just before the outbreak of war, and about the time that 'Battle Dress' was introduced, to the horror of all sartorially conscious officers: many of whom – what an aeon away it seems! – repaired to Savile Row, to have personal Battle Dresses decently cut, rather than don the shapeless official issue.

I had the impertinence to send Creedy a copy of these verses when I wrote them at Sandhurst, just before the war broke out; but I never met him until after it was over, when I made myself known to him in the United Services Club – now no more – in Pall Mall, which he used regularly to frequent. To my enormous gratification, he pulled them, folded and faded, out of his pocket-book, where he assured me they had been throughout the six years since I had sent them to him. He was a dear old boy, who truly loved the Army: which he had loyally served in plain clothes (having been recalled a year after his retirement for the duration of the war in some more junior capacity) for forty-five years, ever since he first joined the War Office in 1901.

Weep, that Sir Herbert Creedy should retire:
    Weep, weep with mighty splashes!
Weep, and put on appropriate attire
    Of Battle Dress and ashes!
How can we hope to win, in our distress,
    New victories, new Megiddos,
Now he has left his children fatherless,
    And has not left us Widdows?

Our parents – nay, our very aunts – might fail
    Sometimes to write us letters,
And even Savile Row might miss a mail
    To their unhappy debtors;
Yet always, 'mid the circulars and bills
    And letters from the needy,
Were pleasant notes, soon fated to be spills,
    Signed by Sir Herbert Creedy.

Gone are those halcyon moments, when he used
    In prose so neat and polished,
To break the news of what was introduced
    And what had been abolished.
What mattered it if he were pleased or pained?
    In terms reserved but fervent,
He would assure us all that he remained
    Our most obedient servant.

Farewell, that correspondence from Whitehall,
    So faithful, so prolific;
Farewell, that far-famed signature, that small
    Familiar hieroglyphic.
Now, unrelieved by him, the duns renew
    Their letters grim and greedy.
We miss him more and more, I'm telling *you*:
    Experto Crede!

For the next few years, like everybody else, I was rather busy; and such scraps of verse as have survived are mostly too topical or too domestic in their allusions to be of interest. I spent most of the war either in the Middle East or in India and Burma. I had two brief spells when I was involved in the Black Art of 'Planning', and in these activities we were diverted from time to time by wholly irrelevant political figures with exotic titles, plotting rebellions or making sinister approaches to our enemies. Pusht-i-Kuh was a mountainous region 200 miles east of Baghdad, just in Iran; Fao was a Sheikdom commanding the western entrance to the Shatt-al-Arab, the name of the broad and strategically important river which results from the confluence of the Tigris and the Euphrates, and flows into the head of the Persian Gulf. The Fakir of Ipi was a fanatical Muslim chieftain who gave trouble in 1942 in a remote corner of what is now Pakistan. For those who might question my scansion, I would make it clear that the stress in the word McGillycuddy comes on the first and the penultimate syllables.

Local Boy
Trying to Make Good

Of all the titles that take my fancy
    At home or here in the Middle East,
Some are as magic as necromancy,
    And all exotic, to say the least.
The Akhoond of Swat I've heard long since of,
    Jerusalem's Mufti intrigues me too;
There's many a place I would fain be Prince of,
    But I'd rather be Wali of Pusht-i-Kuh.

A reigning Duke's an impressive body,
    Lives may hang on a Pasha's smiles,
The Reeks may quake at The McGillycuddy,
    And MacDonald Lord it among his Isles;
Some there be who to win a peerage
    Can think of nothing they wouldn't do:
I would willingly go there steerage
    If I could be Wali of Pusht-i-Kuh.

Dub me now the Fakir of Ipi,
    Offer to make me Sheikh of Fao:
I should remain inert and sleepy,
    Just the same as you see me now.
Lion of Judah? Shah of Persia?
    Paramount Bey of Timbuktoo?
If I'm to be roused from my inertia,
    I must be Wali of Pusht-i-Kuh.

When the war is done, and a grateful nation
    Delights to honour my thoughts of gold,
Parliament's thanks, or a decoration,
    Even a pension leaves me cold.
Let me appear in public places
    And Society papers in '52:
'Snapped with a friend at Goodwood Races:
    The popular Wali of Pusht-i-Kuh.'

Line-Shoot

In January 1945, I became the Military Director of Combined Operations in London, with a flat in King's Bench Walk and an office in Richmond Terrace. For the two previous years, I had been commanding first a Column, and then a Brigade, in Wingate's Special Force behind the Japanese lines in Burma, the 'Chindits'; and it took some time to adjust to the sudden change of scene. Subhas Chandra Bose was the leader of the Indian National Army, which he raised to fight for the Japanese: during the fighting in Burma he was constantly being reported as here, there and everywhere, and it became something of a joke. It may be necessary, after this long passage of years, to remind the reader that 'points' were part of the rationing system: one had certain staple items such as tea, sugar, butter; then there were other items from which you could select, and on these you spent your 'points'. The first line is a quotation from William Dunbar (1465–1530, or thereby). Bouverie Street housed the editorial offices of *Punch*, where these verses appeared early in that happy year.

'London, of townés *a per se . . .*'
   So sang the ancient Scottish poet.
'London's all right,' he meant; and we,
   Back from the Burma jungle, know it.
Yes, every prospect pleases here,
   Life's neither serious nor solemn;
Rice is on points, there's bags of beer,
   And only Nelson's out on Column.

Here is no enemy to baulk,
   I have no need of any sentry;
My bivouac in King's Bench Walk
   Is guarded by a sign: 'No Entry'.
My breakfast I consume in style –
   No need for rice or roots or berries;
My daily march is but a mile
   Along the Thames to Richmond Terrace.

No foes affright, no woes annoy,
   I have no need of compass bearing,
No ambush threatens from Savoy,
   No doubts about the C in Charing;
I do not have to search bamboos
   In Bouverie Street for ration-dropping,
Nor worry over strange canoes
   Reported yesterday from Wapping;

I do not need to make my bed
   In Temple Gardens, nor to build all
My hopes on what that headman said
   (Interrogated at the Guildhall);
I need no guide to Whitehall Court,
   For if perchance I should be lost I'll
Just ask the way: patrols report
   The natives not the least bit hostile;

There are no Japs in Pimlico,
　　Though maybe Subha Chandra Bose is;
The enemy has left Soho,
　　Or so Intelligence supposes;
An agent by the name of Jules,
　　Head waiter at the Purple Heather,
Reliably reports that mules
　　Can use Pall Mall in any weather;

No ants devour my boots at night.
　　No leeches use me as a buffet,
No hungry insects buzz or bite,
　　No spiders stalk me like Miss Muffet.
London is just the place to be:
　　I wouldn't swap with anybody.
The Thames is good enough for me,
　　And you can have the Irrawaddy.

Desiderium

One snag about being on the staff in London in 1945–6 was that one was not allowed a soldier servant, or 'batman'. 'Batman' was the official word, but it was regarded as rather 'common', and normally not used. Staffs had proliferated during the war, and London was swarming with senior staff officers. Service Clubs, in an effort to get back to pre-war standards, began trying to insist on their members being decently dressed.

When first I joined the Army
   In 1931,
Lest anything should harm me
   Some kindly things were done;
Not least of these, I reckoned,
   Was giving me a man
To keep me fairly spick and
   Comparatively span.

That batman was a winner,
   Undaunted, undismayed:
Two ticks to change for dinner,
   One minute for parade!
His skill was never wasted,
   Bis bat qui cito bat,
And never in his case did
   Homerus dormitat.

I reached the age of thirty
   Contented and serene:
At dusk I might be dirty,
   At dawn I would be clean;
No butler offered brandy
   With half the grace that he
Would mix my noon-day shandy
   Or brew my morning tea.

But now those days are over,
  And peace has come to pass,
And I that was in clover
  Am sunk in humble grass;
I labour like a nigger
  That idled yesteryear,
A hapless, piteous figure,
  A London brigadier.

Long since I owned a batman,
  When I was young and svelte;
But now, a middle-aged fat man,
  I clean my boots and belt
With curses and with rudeness,
  With elbow-grease and sweat!
(I have not sunk, thank goodness,
  To Battle Dress as yet).

Farewell, rewards and fairies,
  Good soldiers now may say,
For parrots and canaries
  Fare better far than they:
Birds are made fine by feather
  As in the pre-war years,
But they don't polish leather
  Like London brigadiers.

Black Markets tempt the gluttons
  Who seek exotic fare;
My belt and boots and buttons
  Are like to send me there:
For one Black Market item
  My scruples I would waive,
If I could buy, despite 'em,
  One Nubian Batman-Slave.

Hospitality à la mode

(IN IMITATION OF W. M. PRAED)

In London at that time, it was almost impossible to entertain:
the more so if one had been abroad for several years, and
therefore not on the list of any benevolent grocer or wine-
merchant. For such as I, whisky was unobtainable, gin rare,
and even cheap sherry hard to come by. Certain horrible
substitutes were on offer. The luckless Sir Ben Smith was
Minister of Food.

> You tell me you're coming to see us,
>   My own Araminta, tonight:
> If Bacchus, *ex machina deus*!
>   Delivers some liquor, all right;
> But if we're obliged to make merry
>   On what's in my cupboard, well, then,
> I implore, when I offer you sherry,
>   My own Araminta, say 'When!'

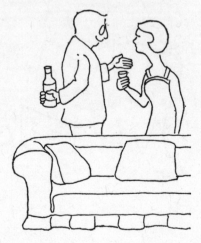

Time was when my man in St James's
    Would offer me liquor galore:
Now one of his principal aims is
    To keep it away from my door.
I can't make him budge an iota
    Though I threaten his life with a Bren:
A bottle a month is my quota –
    My own Araminta, say 'When!'

You may throw all my jam in the gutter,
    You may blue all my 'points' on a 'spread',
You may wolf all my sugar and butter
    And all my nine ounces of bread;
You may offer my sweets to the Vicar,
    You may swear by the shade of Sir Ben,
But when you are offered my liquor,
    My own Araminta, say 'When!'

There is beer – it is long since I mocked ale;
    There is gin – just a couple of nips;
There's a highly inflammable cocktail
    Rightly known as the Five Orange Pips;
There's some brandy left spare from VJ Day
    (You'll see why if you drink and count ten):
If you want to behave like a lady,
    My own Araminta, say 'When!'

Don't wink and suggest that I'm storing
    My bins from Black Market supplies;
Don't pretend not to know when I'm pouring
    And then give a yelp of surprise;
Don't say what the sausages smell like
    And expect to be asked here again;
And let me repeat in your shell-like:
    'My own Araminta, say "When!" '

Application to Join the Secret Service

This was an entry for a competition in the *Spectator*, shortly after the war: one was required to submit such an application in English Sapphics. The setter was an old friend of mine, Richard Usborne, so I had to enter under a pseudonym. I am ashamed to confess that there is a gross lie in the last two lines: I knew Compton Mackenzie very well. But the point was that he was anathema to the security services, having been fined for revealing secrets in his book *Aegean Memories*, and having had his revenge by poking fun at his prosecutors in *Water on the Brain*. When I sent him the verses, he called me a Judas.

Sir: I have cosmopolitan relations;
I was a Language Specialist at Eton;
I have been sacked from many institutions;
    I was at Sandhurst;
I can shoot pips from playing-cards at Bisley;
I am a wow at ciphers and acrostics;
I can drink Vodka, Schnapps and Coca-Cola;
    I was a wet bob;
I can disguise myself as a *suffragi*;
I can speak Hebrew, Dutch and Esperanto;
I can recall the wiles of Mata Hari
    (She was my grand-ma);
I am a blend, in fact, of Peter Wimsey,
Hercule Poirot and Holmes and Lemmy Caution,
And I must add the fact that I do *not* know
    Compton Mackenzie.

WHITEHALL SW1
City OF Westminster

43

Hubble-Bubble

In 1946, I was seconded for a year from the Army, on loan to the Palestine Police as one of their three Assistant Inspectors-General. I had been closely associated with that splendid Force ten years earlier, when I was for a few months Intelligence Officer, Southern Palestine, during the Arab troubles, which were mostly rural. Now they were mostly urban, with bangs and bombs an almost daily occurrence in Jerusalem itself; but many of the older people, like my imaginary Ali (though he derived largely from my imperturbable Sudanese *suffragi* of the same name), remained placid.

Saintly-looking as a Vicar,
  Very old and very sage,
Sitting in his chair of wicker
  Ali contemplates the age.
To and fro, in haste and hurry,
  Go the various sons of Shem:
Ali sits and doesn't worry,
  Looking on Jerusalem.
Peace or riot, truce or trouble,
Ali smokes his hubble-bubble.

British soldiers like the NAAFI,
  Jews the soft and cushioned seat,
Arabs choose the crowded café –
  Ali much prefers the street.
Ali learned the joys of leisure
  In the epoch of the Turk;
Ali knows that perfect pleasure
  Comes from watching others work:
Where the porters pass, bent double,
Ali smokes his hubble-bubble.

When the street is rent asunder
  By the bursting of a bomb,
Ali sits, and doesn't wonder
  Where the noise is coming from.
Fire a rifle or a pistol,
  Ali doesn't bat an eye:
I can see him, clear as crystal,
  When the town goes Hermon-high:
Calm and dusty in the rubble,
Ali smokes his hubble-bubble.

Scottish poets of the late fifteenth and early sixteenth centuries used to indulge in 'Flytings' against each other. The literal meaning of the word is a scolding, but in this sense flytings were an exchange of abusive verses, extremely rude but usually good-humoured. In 1948 the literary editor of the Scottish *Daily Record* induced a few Scottish writers to flyte against each other, and invited me to participate. This was when the writers of the so-called Scottish Renaissance were in full spate, pouring out verse in what they called 'Lallans' or Lowland Scots, which my brother James Fergusson happily dubbed 'Plastic Scots'. This group was apt to regard itself as the true standard-bearer of Scottish literature of mid-century, and tended to mock at those writing in an earlier tradition as 'kail-yarders' – a reference to the despised kailyard school of the turn of the century. The leader and patron saint of the 'Renaissance' was 'Hugh MacDiarmid', or C. M. Grieve, who was so infuriated by the verses that follow that he dashed off two angry pages, which I still have, calling me a liar and a coward.

A Flyting

Frae midden-tap tae midden-tap,
    These Scottish Chauntecleers
Craw loud and lang, and vaunty flap,
    Forbye their wings, their ears.
Shoogling their kaims like cap and bells
    They cry at me and you:
'Ye're a' kailyairders bar oorsels:
    Sing Cock-a-doodle-doo!'
But cocks that only craw at hame
Are aye kailyairders just the same.

The cock that bubbles in the moor,
    The mavis in the trees,
The city sparrow in the stour
    Are worthier bards nor these;
They dinnae seek out unco words
    In unco dictionaries:
They sing their sangs like honest birds –
    Aye, even caged canaries!
As for the kailyaird cock, puir thing,
He craws because he cannae sing.

Vaunty: Boastful   Kaims: Combs
Shoogling: Shaking   Stour: Dust
Unco: Odd

A Ballade of Bereavement

In July 1948, I was commanding the 1st Battalion, The Black Watch, in Germany; and the Colonel of the Regiment, Field-Marshal Lord Wavell (whose father and son were also in The Black Watch) flew over from Aberdeen, which he had been visiting as Chancellor of the University, to spend a few days with us. He brought with him Eric Linklater, the current Rector of the University, who, apart from being a close friend of mine, had been a private soldier in the Regiment on the Western Front during the First World War: the monstrous lie which he had told about his age enabled him to see more than a year's service in the field before his eighteenth birthday. After unpacking, Wavell came downstairs, saying: 'I left my shaving-brush in Aberdeen.' This struck me at once as the perfect key line for a Ballade, of which form of verse he was a keen amateur (witness his 'No Second Front in 1942', which he produced when visiting Moscow with Churchill in that year). We set to work jointly on it that evening, and completed it at the breakfast table the following morning, an occasion described by Linklater in his subsequent book *A Year of Space*. Lines 9–12 and 17–20 were Wavell's, the rest mine, and we fitted them together in their final order over our last cup of coffee. *Timor mortis conturbat* is from Dunbar.

Time was when I was happy and serene
    And mocked at all who thought themselves ill-starred;
Now poltergeists and gremlins intervene
    To haunt and hoist me with my own petard.
    My visit to the Regiment is marred
By a disaster not to be foreseen:
    Timor mortis conturbat, sang the bard –
I left my shaving-brush in Aberdeen.

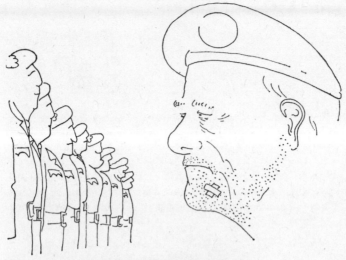

My morning lather is a might-have-been,
  My shaving-soap is like a lump of lard,
My razor is a mockery (though keen) –
  I might as well have used a Pictish shard.
  The harmony of life is sadly marred,
My face has lost its usual ruddy sheen,
  My stubbled cheeks are cicatriced and scarred –
I left my shaving-brush in Aberdeen.

My chin, once glossy as a nectarine,
  Now looks like holly on a Christmas card,
Or straggly hawthorns in a woodland scene
  Such as is deftly drawn by Fragonard.
  No RSM would pass me for a Guard
However much I titivate and preen.
  My luck would daunt a Roland or Bayard:
I left my shaving-brush in Aberdeen.

Pity me, Prince: the water here is hard,
  Hourly my tongue inclines to the obscene.
Full of strange oaths and bearded like the pard,
  I left my shaving-brush in Aberdeen.

The Artless Dodger

In April 1951, I had given up command of my Regiment, and was about to join SHAPE (Supreme Headquarters Allied Powers in Europe), which was then being set up in Paris under General Eisenhower. In the interim, I accepted an invitation from Leonard Russell of the *Sunday Times*, to go to Madrid, witness a bull-fight and write about my reactions. This entailed missing the Census held on the 8th April: hence these lines.

Not for me the Census, not for me the checks:
They don't know whether I'm old or young, my name
                                    or age or sex.
They couldn't ask me posers of all that ever I did,
For I flew away by BEA, and landed in Madrid.

Not for me the buff forms, not for me the queries:
I don't begin to dovetail in to any of their series.
They probably think I did them down, stayed out for
                                    the night, or hid,
But I'll say it again: I went to Spain, and landed in
                                    Madrid.

They don't know how I treat my wife, or earn my
                                    bread and butter,
Whether I live like a howling spiv, or shuffling along
                                    the gutter,
Whether I dodge the Income Tax, or pay whatever I'm
                                    bid:
When they came in swarms to fill the forms, I was
                                    landing in Madrid.

Should I go on their books as the Ace of Crooks, as a
                capitalist or a *rentier*?
Should I figure as which: as Little Tich? Or an outsize
                Georges Carpentier?
Am I known to my friends as Candle-ends, or as Bert,
                or Herb, or Sid? –
They never can tell, for the plane went well, and I
                landed in Madrid.

They don't know what my hobbies are, in spite of their
                statistics –
Numismatics or acrobatics or botany or ballistics;
They don't know whether I'm Gipsy-born, or Scotch, or
                Welsh, or Yid:
It was perfectly fair: I took to the air, and landed in
                Madrid.

They don't know whether I'm dark or fair or smooth
                              or sleek or shaggy;
They don't know whether my eyes protrude, or are
                              sunk, or blind, or baggy;
They don't know whether I'm worth a *sou*, or half a
                              million quid
(Though they probably guess I'm worth much less
                              since landing in Madrid).

It wasn't from pride that I denied these data to Posterity;
If they're not too hurt, I hope to avert any untoward
                              severity.
I'd hate to be racked for my thoughtless act, or roasted
                              on a grid,
Or put in the larder for Torquemada, like they used to
                              do in Madrid.

But not for me the Census, not for me the snoops:
My job was hooked and my passage booked, so I couldn't
                              go through their hoops.
I'd have had to yield in Petersfield or Poole or
                              Pontypridd,*
But I couldn't sign on the dotted line when landing in
                              Madrid.

* But a Welshman wrote, and I beg to quote: 'May you
  roast in Hell beneath!
For Pontypridd doesn't rhyme with squid, it rhymes with
  Edward Heath.'

Lines Written in Dejection

At SHAPE I found myself the senior British member of the
multi-national Intelligence staff. One day Lord Montgomery,
who was Deputy Commander to General Eisenhower, read
an article on the threat to Western Europe by one F. A. Voigt.
He sent for me, and ordered me to travel there and then from
Paris to Bonn, to shew the article to Sir Ivone Kirkpatrick, the
British High Commissioner, and obtain his reactions. Kirk-
patrick thought it very odd, and so did I. It was a boring,
uncomfortable and wholly unnecessary excursion, but I did
not confide this opinion to the Field-Marshal.

How pleasant to know Mr Voigt,
    Who has written such pages of stuff!
He thinks them profound and adroit,
    But I find them annoying enough.

He sits in a beautiful coma
    With nosegays of straw in his hair;
He sniffs a Vansittart aroma,
    But nobody knows that he's there.

He screams, but he cannot Kirkpatrick;
    He casts an impossible quoit:
Ere he fails the first round of his hat-trick,
    How pleasant to know Mr Voigt!

Memorandum from Colonel Fergusson to General Gruenther

General Alfred M. Gruenther was the perfectly splendid Chief of Staff of SHAPE from its first foundation, and the man who really made it work, 'making the rough places plain': he was a great man. He was tough, and you could not take liberties with him; the American officers were frankly frightened of him; but if you stood up to him he quickly became a staunch friend. One morning I received from him a cutting from the London *Times*: *Tutor with Scottish accent urgently required for intelligent parrot. Telephone Chancery 3166.* To this he had attached a note: 'It is my understanding that you intend to apply for this position as an extra-curricular activity. If I can be of any help to you please let me know. I am confident you can handle the job, and will so state.' I locked myself into my office for half an hour to compose a riposte, and my American colleagues were horrified at its frivolity: they awaited a thunderbolt from along the passage. But in fact, General Gruenther had the verses circulated round the Headquarters, and to the American and British press; and sent me a note, which I still have: 'O.K., Bernard, you win! I won't ever tangle with you again.' Bless him: he was and is one of the nicest of men, and far more people are in debt to him for all that he did to establish SHAPE and NATO than realize it.

Brigadier-General Robert A. Schow of the American Army headed the Intelligence Division, with French, Italian and British Deputies: as I have already indicated, I was the British one.

The especially succulent carrot
  That you dangle in front of my eyes
To apply for a job with a Parrot
  Has caused me no little surprise.

I suffer at SHAPE from congestion
  And a change of employment is due,
But I'm hurt that the earliest suggestion
  Should come, General Gruenther, from you.

I'm grateful to know that you'll back me
  For other employment right now,
But certain misgivings still rack me:
  Have you asked the opinion of Schow?

Are you sure it's a job I can handle?
  Are you certain my accent is pure?
Will you swear that there won't be a scandal?
  I repeat once again – are you sure?

There are dangers both serious and solemn
  From which we can scarcely escape:
Could the Parrot comprise a Fifth Column
  Intended to penetrate SHAPE?

Though the dope hitherto is but meagre,
  Precautions are far from absurd:
'Intelligent,' 'Scottish,' and eager –
  There is danger in every word.

Here's a rapidly mounting funicular
  Of things that I don't understand:
My activities extra-curricular
  Perhaps should be rigidly banned.

I used to believe that Intelligence
  Meant life under spurious names,
With a certain admixture of smelly gents
  And a wealth of adorable dames.

Alas! that illusion has vanished:
  I see it was wholly absurd;
But I'm damned if I want to be banished
  From SHAPE to teach Scotch to a bird.

And I now go on record that never
  Do I want to abandon Bob Schow
For a Parrot which, if it were clever,
  Would be talking Scotch anyway now.

In 1955, I arrived in uniform to spend a night with Eric Link-
later, then living in a house called Pitcalzean, near Nigg. On
changing into plain clothes, I found that I had no civilian tie,
and borrowed one of his. In due course, being an honest man,
I returned it with these lines.

Returned with Thanks, One Tie

The Brigadier looks unco trig,
  And weel pit on forbye!
He gaed tae spend a night at Nigg
  And raxed hissel a tie,
For when the hour cam on tae dress
  He hadnae a cravat:
He took his wale of Eric's press,
  And graced hissel wi' that.
O, my! The bonnie tie!
  The brawest in Pitcalzean!
It wadnae daunt a maiden aunt,
  'Twad fair delight a stallion.

The Brigadier gaed doun tae dine,
  Syne up tae seek his bed;
Syne, reinforced wi' champagne wine,
  Fae Eric's yett he sped.
Still brawly buskit see him go –
  Nae bonnier tie on earth!
He wore it at the Highland Show,
  He flaunted it in Perth.
His Adam's apple and ample thrapple
  Ne'er happit were sae trig,
And gey sweir the Brigadier
  Now sends it hame tae Nigg.

Trig: neat	Yett: gate
Weel pit on: well dressed	Buskit: adorned
Forbye: moreover	Thrapple: throat
Raxed: reached for, selected	Happit: wrapped round
Wale: choice	Sweir: reluctantly
Press: cupboard	

Lines in Honour of Professor T. B. Smith

ON THE OCCASION OF HIS BEING APPOINTED QUEEN'S COUNSEL, 1956

Tom Smith, after a hazardous war, some of it behind the enemy lines in Yugoslavia, was from 1949 to 1958 Professor of Scots Law in the University of Aberdeen: which, as every schoolboy ought to know, lies between those two noble rivers, the Don and the Dee. From 1950 to 1955, he also commanded the Aberdeen University Officers Training Corps, in which capacity I was privileged to be his immediate military superior. He accorded to me the minimum of respect and the maximum of friendship.

Henry Cockburn (1779–1854) enshrined for ever in two witty books of social reminiscence, which have become classics, the legal and social world of Edinburgh and Scotland of his day. The first Lord Stair (1619–95) compiled the *Institutes of the Law of Scotland*, and is held in reverence as a law-giver in almost the same league as Moses.

Of Judges and Counsel The Queen has no lack,
For the tides of lawmaking have never run slack;
And always the Sovereign, to keep law and order,
Is in need of advice from both sides of the Border.

In London her Counsel, I'm sorry to say,
Carry on in a very peculiar way,
Indulging at all times in horrible sins:
Black Masses in Temples, and Orgies in Inns.

They reel arm in arm between Fleet Street and Holborn;
They associate Port with the great name of Cockburn;
And – the bars of their Inns never-endingly propping –
They identify Stair with the Old Stairs of Wapping.

These horrible blasphemies none can prevent:
They echo through Essex, they scandalize Kent.
In those honey-combed warrens of villainous vice,
Where on earth can Her Majesty turn for advice?

Thank goodness! the Sovereign can turn in her need
To those wells of pure law-giving north of the Tweed;
And now she's appointed her latest QC.
From the purest of all, to the north of the Dee.

Inter Flumina Faber, sardonic and sage,
Professor and pundit and prop of his age,
The latest Queen's Counsel, in Old Aberdeen;
And the least we can do is sing: 'God Save The Queen!'

The Flyting of the Professors

In 1956 there was an election for the Professorship of Poetry at Oxford, in succession to Professor C. Day Lewis. The three candidates were Sir Harold Nicolson, Professor G. Wilson Knight, and W. H. Auden; Nicolson was the only one I knew. I admired the works of the other two as well; but I thought it was audacious of Auden (who was the successful candidate in the event) to offer himself as a candidate. Admittedly the fact was irrelevant to his quality as a poet or critic; but he had left Britain for the United States when war threatened, and adopted American citizenship: hence the tart final stanza. I had hoped that these verses might appear in *Punch*; but they were rejected by the then editor, Malcolm Muggeridge, for the excellent reason that he had already published a pungent article on the same subject while they were in the post.

The passage of the years may have obscured a few of the allusions. Some of the publishers on the sidelines of the contest were Geoffrey Faber, Rupert Hart-Davis, Jonathan Cape and Mark Longman; John Sparrow, Warden of All Souls, was prominent in the Nicolson lobby; and Professor Wilson Knight had taught at both Dean Close School (Cheltenham) and Stowe.

The Candidates:

We would we were where Lewis lies;
The thought's distracting our bye-byes;
And we're looking at each other with a wild surmise,
    And swiftly diminishing patience.
We're brushing up our Greek as best we can,
And the earliest poetry of Yucatan,
And throwing in our knowledge of *The Brotherhood of Man*
    And also *The Wealth of Nations.*

We're sure we'd stand the strain and stress,
But we're sweating blood a little bit, nevertheless,
And we're reading Mr Cumberlege's Oxford Press
    And his *Dictionary of Quotations*.
Whatever the selection we abide by the election,
    And face the ordeal before us,
And now make way for whatever they may say
    In a Gilbert Murray Greek-style chorus.

Chorus:

Away! for we are ready to a man!
    Our camels smell the fleshpots, and are glad.
Say: Am I Popenjoy or Peter Pan?
    Am I Rubaiyat or Upanishad?
Who is my publisher? The Whatnot Press?
    Geoffrey or Rupert, Jonathan or Mark?
Am I the Reverend Hopkins (modern dress)?
    Am I an Ezra (strictly after dark)?
Away! away! for I will fly to thee,
    Not charioted by Bacchus or his pards,
But on the viewless wings of Subsidy
    (Provided always I can palm the cards).

Voices Off:

'Up, lad!' cries Housman, 'play the Betjeman!
    Gather a fig from out this choice of thistle!'
'Nay, let him carry who can keep the can,'
    Bawls Belloc, from some heavenly Pig and Whistle.
'What *is* he playing at, the Great God Pan,
    Down in Tin Alley?' pipes Lord David Cecil.
Byron, grimacing, says: 'Well, let me see:
Neither a Bowra nor a Spender be.'

Muted Brass, Tympani, Strings and Piccolo:

Black-balls bouncing in the Courts of the Sun;
Remote and ineffectual dons attacking Nicolson;
Tight, white billets-doux like Vallombrosan leaves;
The brawling of a Sparrow (after Yeats) in the eaves.

Recitative:

A Knight comes pricking on the plain
Seeking a ticket on the train
    That puffs by Didcot town.
Know you the secret none can utter?
Half the electors are all a-splutter,
    Telling him: 'You go down.'
Yet he at Oxford long ago
And since by Cheltenham and Stowe
By peaceful rivers soft and slow
Which 'mid the verdant landscape flow,
    Has put Will Shakespeare over:
Himself a Will's son, much enthused –
But not at all to be confused
    With his co-critic, Dover.

Chorus:

Shuffle, shuffle! Huffle duffle!
Dark intrigue, and much kefuffle!
Life is mostly broth and fruffle,
Kindness in another's truffle.

Latinist Arthur Clough uttered a Bridges-like dictum:
  'Feeble and restless youths born to inglorious days.'
Wordsworth might say about foes in the years before
                                    we licked 'em:
  'Some of our writers then dwelt in untreadable ways.'

Verdict for One:

The kiss of the sun for (hic!) Pardon,
  The choice of the bards for mirth:
Rather than nominate Auden,
  We'd have anyone else on earth.

The Duke of Plaza-Toro (1958 Model)

I was still a serving officer, commanding a brigade at Dover, when these verses appeared in *Punch*; and a left-wing Sunday newspaper, now defunct, published a furious article demanding that I should be disciplined for poking fun at such an august body as the United Nations. In the event, all that happened was that I received a frivolous letter from the then Under-Secretary of State for War, encouraging me to write more often.

'The safety of the UN Observers is the first consideration.' (Señor Plaza, Chairman of the United Nations Supervisory Commission in the Lebanon.)

In enterprise of peaceful kind
   For the United Nations,
All thoughts of danger leave behind:
   They lead to complications.
Let frontiers bubble as they will,
   But keep away from Gaza,
      And emulate
      And simulate
      And imitate
      And cultivate
   Your leader, Señor Plaza.
In the first and foremost flight, Ha, Ha!
He arrives upon the site, Ha, Ha!
      Conferring
      In the purring
      And the whirring
         Of the news-reels:
The (former) Duke of Plaza-Toro (now democratized).

And when, to please Dag Hammerskjold,
   You're sent to watch a frontier,
Don't let yourself be over-bold:
   Remember brigands hunt here.
Make sure your airfield's still in touch
   With Nasser's at Almaza:
      Innure yourself,
      Immure yourself,
      Abjure yourself,
      Insure yourself,
   And stick to Señor Plaza.
Whenever something smells, Ha, Ha!
Make sure you're some place else, Ha, Ha!
      You must never
      Be so clever
      As to sever
         Someone's grapevine,
If you are a United Nations Observer.

When warned that you might well be shot
   In carrying out your duty,
Remember poor Count Bernadotte
   And Blankland, Home and Beauty.
Play safe and stick to Beirut beach
   With some indigenous Zsa-Zsa,
      Be sensible,
      Defensible,
      And always indispensable,
   Be safe with Señor Plaza.
To men of grosser clay, Ha, Ha!
He's surely shewn the way, Ha, Ha!
      That captivating
      Calculating
      Pululating
         Personage,
The Chairman of the United Nations Supervisory
   Commission in the Lebanon.

Christmas Day, 1958

Minnie Barnes had already been for years in the service of my wife's family when she took over the job of Nanny in 1915. When she died in her 90s in 1973, independent as ever in her spotless little dwelling among her treasured souvenirs, she had looked after innumerable children and grandchildren. She was for ever coming to the rescue, not least to help out in the various nurseries when the stork was expected at any moment. 'Patrick' was Patrick Campbell-Preston, my exact contemporary at school, at Sandhurst and in The Black Watch, which we joined on the same day. We married sisters (both trained by Minnie); and he succeeded me in command of the Regiment. He was by far my closest friend, and he died in 1960. For Christmas 1958, both families and Minnie were under his hospitable roof, on the shore of Loch Etive in Argyll.

Patrick and I must all our lives
Say: 'Thank you, Minnie!' for our wives.
It's true that ever since we caught them
We wonder how on earth you taught them;
Yet, knowing you, it's not surprising
How keen they are on early rising,
Nor that they know how proud one feels
Of punctuality at meals.
Our eyes with tears are apt to glisten
When we observe them sit and listen:
It really seems almost absurd
The way they hang on every word,
And never seek to be abrupt,
To argue, or to interrupt.
Unlike so many, they're not prone
To gossip on the telephone –
They speak but little, it is true,
And only when they're spoken to.
We owe you thanks for this, dear Min,
And all your nursery discipline.
From Fuffs and Loll it can be seen
How quiet that nursery must have been!

It must have been a wearing life,
Preparing each of us his wife.
Still, you were game for worse things yet,
And one at least we shan't forget:
Though you had gone through such grim hell,
You took their husbands on as well!

A task as difficult as pleasant
Has been to find a Christmas present
For you this year; for every other,
You've caused us all no end of bother.
Whatever we can find for you,
You keep it for a year or two
Safe hidden in some secret store,
Then give it back to us once more!

This year a different situation
Arises, of my own creation:
For once I am constrained to bless
The fruits of my unhandiness.
When you arrived the other day
To stay with us at Ballantrae,
Lifting your case, I broke the straps
Which bound it – an appalling lapse!

And so this year Fate has decreed
There's something that you really need:
    They should be gold,
      They're only leather,
    But they should hold
      Your case together:
    When next I lift
      It up on top,
    I hope my gift
      Won't let it drop.
May they hold fast and ne'er unravel;
May they enable you to travel
Between Loch Etive and the Clyde
And all your other homes beside.
They and their children welcome you,
And all their children's children too.

There is one gift besides all these:
You must accept it, if you please:
A gift to which you can't say 'Nay',
Though you may lock it fast away.
Accept it, and don't make a fuss:
LOVE AND GOOD LUCK FROM ALL OF US!

For Bill Luce

After twenty-six years in the Sudan and five as Governor of Aden, Sir William Luce was created GBE in the New Year Honours of 1961, and appointed Political Resident, Persian Gulf, in the same week.

How pleasant it must be to be
PRPG and GBE,
To know one's name will soon inspire
Deep-seated terror in Bushire.
'*Allah yehfazkum!*' they will mutter
With reverence in the *suqs* of Qatar,
Or mew it like a frightened puss-cat
In Mohammerah or in Muscat.
Mothers scare children in Dhahran
With tales of 'Luce of the Sudan'.
Your name and fame must bulk still larger
In Abu Dhabi and in Sharja,
Scaring the wickedest old-timer
In Ajman or in Ras-al-Khaimah,
Yielding in precedence to no man
Throughout the length of Lucial Oman.
Mabrouk! Mabrouk in this New Year
To you, Sir William *El Kebir*.

Allah yehfazkum: May God avert the arrow
Mabrouk: Congratulations
El Kebir: The Great

The Sidewalks of New York (1970 Version)

For several years, Dr Horace Donegan, the then Bishop of New York, was an annual visitor to Royal Lodge, Windsor, as a guest of Her Majesty Queen Elizabeth The Queen Mother; and an informal, light-hearted croquet series was a regular feature, with much the same players each year. It will be remembered that in *Alice in Wonderland* live flamingos did service as croquet mallets. *The Sidewalks of New York*, of which the opening line was 'East Side, West Side, all around the Town,' was a political song in support of a popular Mayor of New York in the early 1920s.

East Side, West Side, all around the lawn,
See them playing Croquet, Queen and Bishop, Knight
and Pawn.
Watch the Bishop cheating with a special kind of
torque –
All the tricks they've taught him on the Sidewalks of
New York.

East Side, West Side, rolling down the slope:
Bishop shews no Charity, no Faith, and little Hope.
Stop the Bishop swearing, though this may require a
cork:
Gosh! What words they've taught him on the Sidewalks
of New York!

East Side, West Side, all the afternoon
The Bishop's game's improving, and he'll be a
champion soon.
Perhaps 'twas a flamingo, and not the usual stork,
That dumped a Baby Bishop on the Sidewalks of New
York.

Medicine Men

Early in 1970, after various travels abroad, I contracted that unpleasant tropical disease Sprue. Fortunately for me, I fell at once into good hands, who diagnosed the trouble swiftly and correctly. To begin with, there were three of them, whom I christened 'The Three Jovial Ghouls'; and with them I had many jolly discussions as to whether the trouble was in the Rectum, the Colon, or elsewhere: and whether the Surgeon or the Physician should have the last word. Later on, The Three Ghouls (Sir Francis Avery-Jones, Sir Clifford Naunton Morgan and Sir Ralph Southward) were joined by a fourth, Professor Alan Woodruff, who succoured me two years later when I had a burst appendix – which is an entirely different story. But from those seven weeks in hospital in London in March and April of 1970, there stemmed these two sets of immortal verse.

I

They belong to the kindest of schools,
My trio of Jovial Ghouls:
　　They prescribe for my ills
　　The most succulent pills,
And take a delight in my stools.

74

II

If I'm losing some Lower Intestine
    (And I hope it's in feet, not in miles)
Its ultimate home I would destine
    A suitable plot in Saint Giles.
Be it Rectal or Home-and-Colonial,
    I suggest that its ultimate fate
Be attended by due ceremonial,
    And as such recognized by the State.

I think I would harbour a grievance
    If treated as anything less:
Lord Lyon and all his Pursuivants
    Must be there in appropriate dress;
And when we hand over the gristle
    Or tripe or whatever it be,
Make sure that the Dean of the Thistle
    Is there, and none other than he.

Imagine: the Pipers are playing,
    The Soldiers are lining the street,
The Medical Students are braying
    (Or such other noise as is meet);
The Golfers at Muirfield are cursing
    And missing their ultimate putt,
And the Dean of the Thistle is nursing
    This relic of Fergusson's gut.

Forget all extraneous topics;
    Forget all the treatment I've had;
Forget all my years in the Tropics
    And my carryings-on, good and bad;
Forget my field-cooking and mess-tin,
    Forget swollen feet and the piles,
But remember the day my Intestine
    Was duly laid up in Saint Giles.

Nightmare

At 3 a.m. on 17 January 1971 (which, incidentally, would have been my Father's 106th birthday if he had been alive) I woke up with these words running in my head: 'My Mother's Mother was a Hunter Blair.' This is perfectly true; and my Father always maintained that any eccentricities which might emerge in his offspring would derive from that fact: this could well be true too. There is no particular point in these verses, except that they are factual, even to the names of my seven great-uncles; and the Hunter Blairs have been our neighbours for several centuries, and have inter-married with my own family more than once. Blairquhan is the ancestral home where the Hunter Blairs lurk.

I know that I am something of a Square,
  Belonging to a pattern mostly gone:
A type that nowadays is found nowhere,
  Unless it be in Butler's *Erewhon*.
  I contemplate the world like Solomon
In brooding wisdom verging on despair,
  But still I boast some sort of colophon:
My Mother's Mother was a Hunter Blair.

Ayrshire's a County where you stand and stare –
  There's always some unique phenomenon:
No need for *Oh, Calcutta!* or for *Hair!*:
  We've always some excitement going on.
  A lecture on Scotch Missions in Ceylon,
An outing to the Cinema in Ayr,
  Or Ludo in the precincts of Blairquhan:
My Mother's Mother was a Hunter Blair.

I've had some uncles who were rather rare:
  My Uncles Davie, Eddie, Fobbie, Don,
And Walter, Reggie, Gilbert, who bid fair
  To fill a whole and vast Pantechnicon!
  How this affects the politics of Bonn
Or Common Market's neither here nor there:
  The fact remains – and this is always fun –
My Mother's Mother was a Hunter Blair.

  Envoi

Prince! You're a snob! The type I spit upon!
  And probably a bogus one: Beware!
Although I may be neither 'De' nor 'Von',
  My Mother's Mother was a Hunter Blair.

Lines in Honour of George MacLeod

ON THE FIFTIETH ANNIVERSARY OF HIS ORDINATION

I have known George MacLeod, *alias* The Very Reverend Lord MacLeod of Fuinary, MC, DD, since I was seventeen years old; he was then Minister of Govan. After schooling at Winchester and a distinguished war-time career in The Argyll and Sutherland Highlanders, he was ordained in the ministry of the Church of Scotland towards the end of 1924. We have been friends and adversaries, disagreeing on many subjects. He has long been, among many other things, a pacifist and a champion of 'liberation' causes in Africa. In 1938 he founded the Iona Community; in 1957 he was elected Moderator of the General Assembly of the Church of Scotland; in 1967, already by inheritance a baronet, he was made a life peer. He once defeated me on a motion in the General Assembly by the triumphant margin of 1200 votes to 50, or thereby. Shortly before Christmas 1974, the Presbytery of Glasgow honoured him on his Jubilee as a minister; and without my knowledge, but to my great gratification (and without any fore-knowledge on his part) these verses, which he had not previously seen, were read out on that occasion.

(*Tune: Down Ampney*)

Clap hands for George MacLeod!
No noise could be too loud
   From Govan Kirk to Canongate resounding.
Ye mountains and ye isles,
Ye 91st Argylls,
   Frelimos all, proclaim his grace abounding.

For every evil, sure,
He can prescribe a cure,
    For every ill his own specific nostrum;
Assembly every year
Receives him 'loud and clear',
    And cheers him warmly as he leaves the rostrum.

I don't infer by this
That life is perfect bliss
    When he at last achieves his peroration:
When George gets up to speak,
Debates, however bleak,
    Transform themselves into a constellation.

For him the fresh approach,
For him new walls to broach,
    New ears to hear with, and new eyes to see with.
No matter that each time
With confidence sublime
    He thunders theories that I can't agree with.

Today among his Peers
Wisdom of fifty years
    Brings vintage from a ripe and rich distilling:
Still challenging and tough,
Provocative and rough,
    But ours for many years to come, God willing.

He links both black and white,
He straddles Left and Right,
    Impersonating, so to speak, an isthmus.
And so with heart and voice
His friends today rejoice,
    And wish both him and his a Happy Christmas.

The Crest on the Silver

No particular date attaches to these lines, which appeared in a special number of *Punch* during the editorship of Malcolm Muggeridge, entitled *Snoblesse Oblige*. At the material time, L. G. Pine was the editor of *Burke*. As a matter of interest to me, if to nobody else, my great-great-grandfather was the Judge at the trial of Burke and Hare in the 1820s.

To every poor relation
  Where'er his lot be cast,
The annual invitation
  To disinter his past.
The post has brought the flimsy
  Proof-sheets to con with care:
Let us indulge the whimsy
  Of Burke, if not of Hare.

In verbiage monumental
  Are logged in tomes immense
Landowners not so gentle,
  And not-so-landed gents.
Should economic blizzards
  Distress a noble line,
Let them control their gizzards,
  And peak, but not re-Pine.

However wide the rift is
  Between the twig and tree,
Still in the nineteen-fifties
  Thrives Genealogy.
The Family's last ember
  Is not extinguished yet:
Haply we may remember,
  But surely will Debrett.

For Sir Miles Clifford on his 80th Birthday, 1977

Much of Miles Clifford's career was in Nigeria, but he was Colonial Secretary of Gibraltar for two years during the war, and Governor of the Falkland Islands from 1946 to 1954. He was subsequently on the LCC, and on the Council of the Royal Geographical Society.

Ring the bells from every steeple
    O'er the continents and isles:
Every sort of curious people
    Shout the praises of Sir Miles!
If you need a good placebo
    For an angry Mick or Scot,
Falkland Islander or Ibo,
    Clifford can placate the lot.
Scourge of indolent officials
    From the top of many a tree;
Keen collector of initials –
    RGS to LCC.
Give him Hymnary or Psalter,
    He will lead the Psalms and Hymns:
In the war, the Rock, Gibraltar,
    Trembled at his lightest whims.
Awful thought, but one supposes
    It would scarcely have been odd
Had Miles Clifford, *à la* Moses,
    Rent Gibraltar with a rod.

                    ★

Everybody knows a leaven
    Is required to right the lump:
Vintage 1897
    Takes the wicket, middle stump.
I am sad – my luck is hellish –
    That I'm stuck in Ballantrae,
But I'll drink your health with relish,
    Even *in absentia*.

For my Great-Nephew
Iain Fergusson

ON THE OCCASION
OF HIS BAPTISM

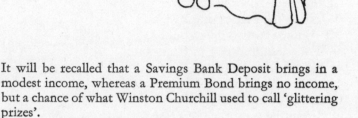

It will be recalled that a Savings Bank Deposit brings in a
modest income, whereas a Premium Bond brings no income,
but a chance of what Winston Churchill used to call 'glittering
prizes'.

Dear Iain: I am very fond
Of what they call 'The Premium Bond',
   An admirable invention,
For long before you're very old
These paper sheets will turn to gold –
   Or such is the intention.

When in due course you win a prize
You will no doubt, with startled eyes,
   Ask your Papa: 'What was it?'
As I foresee the happy scene,
He will reply: 'It might have been
   A Savings Bank Deposit;

'It might have been, upon my oath,
Investment with a steady growth,
   And good for bread and butter.
This would have been far wiser, yet
Your old great-uncle liked to bet,
   And dearly loved a flutter.

'And so, my boy, it's thanks to him
And to his horrid gambling whim
    (A born star-waggon-hitcher)
That this well-omened day has come,
And brought you this enormous sum,
    To make us all much richer.

'So now, to celebrate your wealth,
We'll drink Great-Uncle Bernard's health
    (Pray do not call him "Bernie");
And coupled with him, as we ought,
We'll spare an extra kindly thought
    For benefactor Ernie.'

So do not let your parents spoil
This gushing of potential oil
    By Savings Bonds, or such-like:
In Premium Bonds let them invest,
And let Dame Fortune do the rest
    And use the Midas Touch, like.

And talking of potential oil,
Do not mislay the counter-foil:
    That would indeed be dismal!
It's early days to think of thrift,
But tuck beneath your bib this gift,
    This happy day baptismal.
Conceal it in the robe of lace
    You're wearing for the christening.
(Tell no one of its hiding-place –
    Your Grand-Pa might be listening).

In September 1972, I was dawdling through various countries of South-East Asia on my leisurely way to Hong Kong. In the course of the journey, I imposed myself on Barry Smallman, then Counsellor at the British Embassy at Bangkok: we had known each other in previous incarnations a few years earlier, when I was Governor-General of New Zealand and he the British Deputy High Commissioner. (It was while I was in Bangkok that I received a cable inviting me to become Chairman of the British Council, an invitation which I joyfully accepted.) My next port of call was to be Saigon, where I was to stay with the New Zealand Ambassador, Sir Leonard Thornton, and to lunch with the Foreign Minister, an old friend called Tran Van Lam; but at Bangkok Airport I suffered the humiliation of finding that my visa was not in order: indeed, I had no visa at all. So I missed the aircraft; had to postpone the luncheon for twenty-four hours; and was obliged to return with my tail between my legs to Barry Smallman's house, and ask for a further night's lodging for myself and my A.D.C., which he generously accorded.

I testify with my hand on my heart that he knocked off these elegiacs, sitting at his desk in my presence and without recourse to a dictionary, in eight minutes flat. The last eight words refer to a volume of autobiography which I had just published, under the title *The Trumpet in the Hall*. His verses come first, followed by a rough translation; then my riposte.

A Taste of Latinity

O Fergi fili, voluisti evadere frustra,
  Dis aliter visum: visa maligna fuit.
Currusque aetherius (miserum!) vis tale superbum
  Infirmis pennis ferre nequibat onus.
Quid nunc auxilium? quae nunc spes, miles? In aula
  Olim terribilis nunc tuba muta latet.

O Son of Fergus, you wished in vain to depart
  Heaven rules otherwise, your visa was unkind.
And your airborne chariot (the dirty dog!) which looked
                                              so good
  Refused to carry its load on uncertain wings.
What help now? What hope now, soldier? In the Hall
  The once terrible Trumpet now lies mute.

Reply to Smallman

Too rare to lose, their quality unmatched,
Homunculus's verses are attached.
Let others strive, in London or Bangkok,
To emulate his efforts, all *ad hoc.*
Let others seek the target, hit or miss:
Homunculus is *sui generis.*
Encouraging the downcast where despair is,
Homunculus is *primus inter pares.*
Let people damn the tall by innuendo:
Homunculus? Lucus a non lucendo.
His colleagues? He pronounces nothing on 'em
Till qualified to say '*Nil Nisi Bonum.*'
Of all his many diplomatic tricks, I
Prefer *Et Ego in Arcadia Vixi.*
As for my thwarted flights, the best I can do
May well turn out *Solvitur Ambulando.*

For Tony Parsons

In the New Year Honours of 1975, a few weeks after we had been staying with him, the British Ambassador to Iran was made KCMG. Before transferring to the Diplomatic Service some twenty years earlier, he had been a colonel in the Royal Artillery.

Being rather a snob with an eye for a job,
    For a General's pips or an Admiral's stripe-line,
I am always delighted whenever I've sighted
    An obvious KCMG in the pipe-line.

As often as not, I find that my shot
    Has failed to connect, and results in a runner;
But this time at least I have slaughtered the beast
    And can put in my Gamebook; 'One broken-down
                            Gunner'.

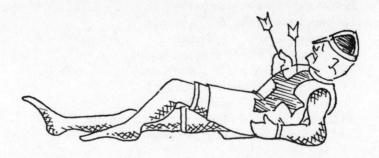

Though Heaven may rage at the ills of the age,
    There is always rejoicing in regions infernal:
What more could delight the Powers of the Night
    That a K for a former Artillery Colonel?

Hitch wagon to star for cheap caviar,
    And claim to drink vodka for free, *nolens volens*:
While Ambassadors gorge, to Saints Michael and George
    I felt bound to address a short note of condolence.

Their answer's just come: it has stricken me dumb!
    It has just been deciphered, and reads: 'O, Boloney!
We've waited an age for Tony's next stage.
    Please tell him the Gin's on the boil. Love to Tony.'

So what can I do but offer to you
    My personal plaudits, in such a dilemma?
We don't want a reply, but Laura and I
    Send greetings to you, and to Pam, and to Emma.

H.B.–G   89

Ballade of the Bath

(DEDICATED TO PROFESSOR CONSTANTINE TRYPANIS, DLitt, FRSL)

During my travels as Chairman of the British Council, I met many old friends and made many new ones. Among these last was Professor Trypanis, long resident in Oxford, but at this period Minister of Culture in the Greek Government. While acting as host to my wife and me at a dinner party in Athens, he told me that be had just been back to Oxford for a conference, and had found himself billeted for its duration in Lady Margaret Hall, a women's college. 'I never expected any such thing,' he said, 'but I had a bath in Lady Margaret Hall.' As in the matter of Lord Wavell (see page 9), the cadence of the words struck me, and the resultant Ballade was inevitable. I am happy to say that he was delighted with it.

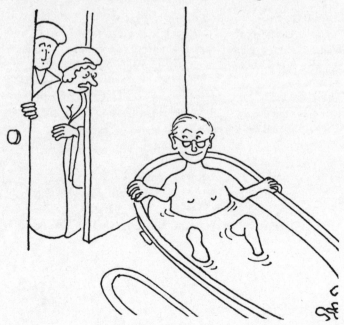

Adam and Eve looked fine before the Fall,
  He like Apollo, she like Artemis:
They suffered no embarrassment at all –
  They didn't even wear a Golden Fleece.
  They never risked the wrath of the Police,
So life was dull, and soon began to pall,
  As mine did, till, while visiting from Greece,
I had a bath in Lady Margaret Hall.

If one divided in three parts, like Gaul,
  Or sought from Delphi tips for one's release,
Or found conversion on the road, like Saul,
  Then life's no more a jail, but perfect peace.
  It's handy, I admit, to have a niece
Or other relative beyond the wall,
  But I have realized my chief caprice:
I had a bath in Lady Margaret Hall.

We're all alike: the stunted and the tall,
  The bright, the dull, the skinny, the obese;
But our ambitions vary, and the call
  Bewilders us, as though we were but geese.
  Abou Ben Adhem (may his tribe increase)
Enjoyed himself – he had the wherewithal:
  Like a French audience, I cry: '*Bis, Bis!*'
(I had a bath in Lady Margaret Hall).

Prince, on my mind's no painful cicatrice:
  I feel like Cinderella at the Ball!
Now I can wait, content, for my decease:
  I had a bath in Lady Margaret Hall.

Ode to the Hamper

(ORIENT EXPRESS, MARCH 1976)

I had long nurtured a desire to travel on the Orient Express, and achieved this ambition with my wife about a year before it finally expired. We had been warned that all the glory had long since left it. We were the only passengers travelling all the way from Istanbul to Paris, and throughout those three long days only one hot meal was provided: a single and very expensive luncheon between Venice and Milan. But thanks to the local knowledge and the hospitable instincts of the Istanbul staff of the British Council we were furnished with an enormous hamper, full of goodies. Its contents enabled us to sustain ourselves, and to give an occasional hand-out to others with less foresight, all the way from the Bosphorus to the Seine.

Should you ever wish to travel
    On the Orient Express,
There's no problem to unravel
    Re provisions for the Mess:
There's a secret incantation
    Known to esoteric cults
Which will crown your application
    With astonishing results.

There's been dark and secret knowledge
    Almost since the world was born
Deep secreted in a College
    Somewhere on the Golden Horn.
If you asked the proper person
    He would grant you what you wished:
He would put a lovely curse on –
    Or a sturgeon, if you fished.

Both voluptuary and votive,
    Diabolic or divine,
Thus achieved their dearest motive:
    Canonized, or concubine.
Catalogue or manifesto
    Read with minimum of fuss:
Chant the words, and then – Hey, Presto!
    Joy upon the Bosphorus!

See the Council Chairman scamper
    With the wife to whom he's yoked
To investigate the Hamper
    Which the magic spell invoked.
Veritable double-decker
    Suitable for the rotund:
Sort of thing James Elroy Flecker
    Might have sent to Samarkand.

Port and chicken, tea and coffee,
  Cake and shortbread, cheese and jam,
Rolls and butter, *loukoum,* toffee,
  Fried potato chips and ham,
Wine and whisky, beer and *raki,*
  Knives and forks and teaspoons too,
Plates and cups and – aren't we lucky? –
  Lots of paper for the loo.

What, then, is this incantation?
  Obviously my lips are sealed.
For some huge consideration
  It might haply be revealed.
What I know beyond all question
  Is that no one but a fool
(Or from fear of indigestion)
  Hamperless would leave Stamboul.

For Mistress Peggy Kirk, MBE

In May, 1975, the new Strathclyde Region gobbled up the old Ayrshire County Council, on which Mrs Kirk, member of an ancient family in the parish, had represented Ballantrae for many years; travelling to every nook and cranny of the county by public transport, and a doughty champion of every worthy cause. Messrs Paterson and Hair were respectively the County Convener and County Clerk.

> In Ballantrae this unco day
>   Our fate we cannae shirk;
> Nae ferlie that our herts are wae –
>   We're losin' Mistress Kirk.
>
> She terrorized the bureaucrat
>   As wi' a bluidy dirk:
> They'd scriech: 'O dinnae threaten that!
>   Cry back your Mistress Kirk!'
>
> Oppose her, and she'd warsle back
>   As essart as a stirk;
> And yet, nane kinder for a crack
>   Than Mistress Peggy Kirk.
>
> She'd travel a' the county wide
>   Fae early morn till mirk:
> Nae problem o' the kintra-side
>   Could fickle Mistress Kirk.
>
> Schules, hooses, hospitals – or drains –
>   Nae problem seemed tae irk:
> Young mairrit folk, auld wifies, weans
>   Were bairns tae Mistress Kirk.

We cannae bide this new Strathclyde,
But wish it weel whate'er betide.
Thon matter's neither here nor there,
But of ae thing we're all aware:
That Mistress Kirk is kin' o' spare.
She'll no be bussin aye tae Ayr
In weather coorse or saft or sair
Tae fecht our battles, do and dare
And beard sic bodies in their lair
As Messrs Paterson and Hair.
(In future, she'll maun pay the fare,
But as tae that she willnae care.)
In these daft days, ae thing is shair,
    So why should we be wae?
She's back amang us evermair,
    Back hame in Ballantrae.

Unco: (in this sense) exceptional   Essart: obstinate
Ferlie: wonder   Crack: chat
Wae: sorrowful   Mirk: darkness
Warsle: (in this sense) fight   Fickle: baffle

Lord Love a Duck

Bernard and Laura, two Paradise Duck from New Zealand named after my wife and myself, were introduced and acclimatized on Tresco, in the Isles of Scilly. Although their union was duly blessed, they rejected their offspring, who had to be found a foster-mother in Mrs Cooper's hen-run: a highlight of 1976.

All's quiet in the City;
    No tidings from UNESCO;
No Cricket, more's the pity –
    But thrilling news from Tresco!
In jorums (or in jora?)
    Drink deep, and not in siplets,
For Bernard, yes, and Laura
    Have just indulged in triplets!

But Laura doesn't love them:
    They have to be adopted.
To put a roof above them
    The Coopers were co-opted.
The Tresco plot thus thickens:
    I'd heard of Swans called Whoopers,
Of Mother Carey's Chickens,
    But *never* Mother Cooper's.

Lines Written in Heartfelt Gratitude to Ian McClure, Esq., FRCSE

ON THE OCCASION OF THE QUEEN'S
JUBILEE SERVICE IN GLASGOW CATHEDRAL
17 MAY 1977

While dressing for this memorable service, which I was required to attend as a member of the Order of the Thistle, I made the discovery so familiar to me from nightmares: I had no braces, and all the shops were shut. Fortunately I was staying in Ayr, and I threw myself on the mercy of my Ear, Nose and Throat specialist: who came to my rescue, and not for the first time by a long chalk.

The dawn rose bright on Ayr this morning,
　　Till suddenly it turned full dour:
There came a sort of Gypsy's Warning
　　Like haar upon the Lammermuir.
Hark at the doom the Warlock speaks:
'Ye hae nae braces for yer breeks!'

Now what's to do? for *absit omen*:
　　The outlook's very far from sound.
I can't rely on my abdomen
　　To keep my trousers off the ground,
And like as not the wind will whistle
About my legs beneath the Thistle.

I'll cause the most Almighty scandal
　　In the Cathedral, that's for sure.
The only person who can handle
　　My situation is McClure.
I'm certain he will succour me,
Though it's not strictly ENT.

★

Up the Cathedral aisle I wended
　　My dignified and glorious way.
Least said, we know, is soonest mended,
　　So thanks for all your help today.
Your braces held my breeks suspended:
　　They stood, and Earth's foundations stay:
　　　So,
　　　　Yours sincerely
　　　　　Ballantrae.

Trivia

I

I'm a Lucky Chap
(Coronation Week, 1937)

I met a man
From Yucatan,
   Home for the Coronation,
Who's told me how
To make 'A Thou,' –
   It's not a speculation.
He's found untold
Reserves of gold:
   I don't know where, precisely;
But I invest,
He does the rest!
   That ought to do me nicely.

II

The Lower Classes are such fools,
They waste their money on the pools.
I bet, I know; but that's misleading:
One must encourage bloodstock breeding.

III

(On being told that the new owner of *The Times*
newspaper was coming to call)

Lord Thomson of Fleet
Was sick in the street:
The most heinous of crimes,
But a sign of *The Times*.

IV

The Devil, having nothing else to do,
Went off to tempt the Inland Revenue.
The Tax Collector, guessing it was he,
Devised a special Form called Schedule D.
The Devil countered with a merry quip,
Since when the two have been in partnership.

STIRLING
DISTRICT
LIBRARY

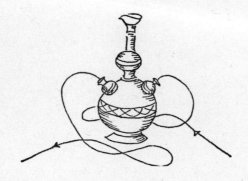